ST. ANDREW'S, ST. ANDREWS

An episcopal congregation
1689 to 1993

Some historical notes

John Thompson

Published in 1994

by

Hutton Press Ltd,
The Old Manse,
Queen Street,
Tayport,
Fife DD6 9NS

ISBN 1 872167 61 6

Printed by:

Geo. E. Findlay & Co. Ltd.
Larch Street, Dundee DD1 5NW

Cover illustration: Saint Andrew's Church shortly before the
removal of the tower and spire, c.1930.

PREFACE

In 1896 T.T. Oliphant closed the 19th Century with his history of Saint Andrew's Church. Those who know that volume will recognise Oliphant was writing at the peak of Episcopal building programmes. Dr. John Thompson, closing the 20th Century, has seen those grandiose programmes ease into a more responsible missionary framework for the church. He has seen also the secularising revolution of the 1960's and despite uncertainty of the eventual outcome of this revolution has seen the congregation he loves grow.

Dr. Thompson has produced for us a fine and extremely readable history of Saint Andrew's Church. He has at times with gentle wit found the lighter side of the congregation's life. At other times he has with quietly disguised but nevertheless stern seriousness criticised for failures both of omission and commission. And yet no one could but fail to warm to what has been written with such tender insight.

In this little book he has provided a window for readers to look into the life of this historic congregation. Dr. Thompson writes in the great tradition of Oliphant.

R.A. Gillies
St. Andrews, November 1993.

ACKNOWLEDGEMENTS

For sources of information I am grateful to Mr. J.L. Hunter Scott, the vestry clerk, who put at my disposal the minutes of the vestry, which go back to 1825, and to successive rectors, the Reverend R.T Halliday (now the Rt. Reverend Bishop of Brechin) and the Reverend Dr. R.A. Gillies who both unearthed much unexpected material. To their names I should add that of Mr. I.D. Gilroy who found more material when he was clearing the rectory before its division.

Mr. R.N. Smart, Keeper of the University Muniments allowed me to keep this material in the University archives, and over the years has proved a patient and never–failing answerer of questions. From Dr. R.G. Cant's ecclesiological learning I have learned much about church architecture and forms and traditions. Mr. G. Christie has been very helpful in answering my questions about the town, which he knows so well, and its inhabitants.

Many senior members of the congregation have given me help by recalling happenings during their membership. Two, in particular, must be named. Mr. Melville Reid and Mr. Jimmy

Ireland, have been devoted servants of the church from boyhood to their present maturity. During these long years they have acquired an intimate knowledge of the church, of its furnishings and of the people who have filled the pews.

Lastly I must acknowledge my debt to the late T.T. Oliphant. His "Historical Notes relating to the Episcopal Congregation of St. Andrews from the time of the Revolution to the present day, 1896" is a model of what a church history should be. I have plundered it.

The photographs used are copies of photographs in the University Library collection and are reproduced here by permission of the librarian.

INTRODUCTION

The year 1689 is commonly given as the date of the beginning of the Episcopal Church, but this gives a misleading impression. It suggests that the Episcopal Church began as a sect which split away from the main stream of the Church of Scotland in that year because of doctrinal difficulties. In fact the first episcopal congregations formed round those ministers of the Church of Scotland, the great majority of the ministers of the Church of Scotland, who had been forced to leave their charges and their livings for political reasons. They did not consider themselves to be sectarians, but rather "the faithful remnant" of the Church of Scotland, faithful because they remained loyal both to episcopacy and to their exiled king.

For most of the 17th century until 1689 the Church of Scotland was episcopal in its form of government with bishops appointed after the royal conge d'elire. Once appointed they had considerable political power, forming the first of the three estates of parliament, as well as exercising power through the ecclesiastical courts. This system of church government was repugnant to a large minority within the church, including some of the ablest churchmen of the time. To them the control of the Church by the

Crown through bishops was abhorrent. They struggled to replace episcopal rule by presbyterianism. We could liken the 17th century church to a modern parliament where a large and influential opposition seeks to gain control of the government.

From 1638 to 1661, the years of the Bishops' Wars, the Civil War and the Protectorate, the presbyterian party controlled the Church. The restoration of Charles II brought the restoration of episcopacy but left a presbyterian party strengthened by years of power and by its alliance with English presbyterians during the Civil War. In the south west of Scotland and in many of the burghs of the Lothians and Fife anti–episcopal, presbyterian feeling was strong, so strong that it led on occasion to armed insurrection and often to public worship in conventicles away from the parish church. The accession of James VII in 1685 strengthened anti–episcopal feeling, for he was an avowed Roman Catholic and the prospect of bishops being nominated by him was disturbing.

In the end the form of government of the established church in Scotland was determined by politics. In 1688 King James was forced to flee from England after the invasion of William of Orange. His flight left a political vacuum in Scotland. The Scottish bishops, through Bishop Rose of Edinburgh, made it plain to William that they held themselves bound by their oaths of loyalty to King James and could not recognise him as rightful king. William was forced to look for support in Scotland to those magnates who, out of conviction or hope of power, supported the presbyterian party. He found that support in a Convention which met in Edinburgh in the spring of 1689, a Convention where the lowland burghs were well represented but the lands north of the Tay poorly represented.

The Convention lost no time in beginning an ecclesiastical revolution. On April 4th it declared that James had forfeited the crown. A week later it offered the crown to William and Mary, accompanying the offer with a document, the Claim of Right, which asserted that "Prelacy and superiority of any office in the Church above presbyter is, and hath been, a great and unsupportable grievance and trouble in this nation and contrary to the inclinations of the generality of the people .... and therefore ought to be abolished." On April 13th all clergy were ordered to pray for William and Mary as king and queen of Scotland. Those who failed to do so risked losing their benefices. The majority refused. In St. Andrews the two ministers of Holy Trinity Church were Archdeacon Richard Waddell and John Wood. Both were summoned before a committee of the Estates on the 11th of May 1689 and required to take the oath of loyalty to William and Mary and to abjure King James. Both refused and were deprived. We could consider that date as the date when the Episcopal Church of Scotland in St. Andrews became disendowed and disestablished with no church to meet in and no fixed stipend for its clergy.[1]

CHAPTER I

At the time of his eviction from Holy Trinity Church Dr. Waddell was already a minister of wide experience. He had held charges in Stenton, Dunbar, Kelso and Glasgow before coming to St. Andrews. His ministry in St. Andrews to those who followed him out of the new establishment was not without interruptions. He was banished from the town in 1691 but returned later. In 1703 letters of horning were raised against him at the instance of the agent of the established church, ordering him "to remove forth of the town and parochine of St. Andrews and not to return thereto". He was succeeded by the Reverend G. Mathers who was also forced to leave St. Andrews in 1706. He died in Edinburgh soon afterwards. Waddell came back later and from 1712 or earlier till his death in 1718, ministered to the faithful remnant. "Having performed all the duties of a good and upright man he died in St. Andrews 89 years old on the 11th of June 1718 to be gathered to his fathers, a catholic priest, the husband of one wife", as his long, Latin epitaph ends.[2]

He was not alone in serving the episcopal community. Wodrow in his "Analecta" includes a letter from a Mr.

Haddo, presumably Professor Hadow, of St. Mary's:

"Mr. Haddo, at St. Androues, tells me there are at
S.Androues severall of the outed clergy; and one
Strachan who has the English service. His
congregation, it seems, was not very numerouse;
and, therefore, he came and joyned with
Archdeacon Waddell, and when, upon the
Toleration, Waddell began and prayed for the
Queen and Hannover, they separated again, and
set up a distinct meeting, with the English service.
Lately, he tells me, Forsyth was reading prayers; I
doe not (know) whither on trick or by oversight,
he read the Petitions for Queen Anne and Sophia
the most part of his hearers in testimony of their
not joyning, sate down in the time, and rose again
when that was over. Serverall of them came and
compleaned heavily to him, and threatened to
leave him. He answered, it was a mistake, and
the book had led him to it".

Two phrases in the extract are significant for the future
history of the congregation – "the English service" and
"prayed for the Queen and Hannover".

The liturgy of 1637[3] was not used after the restoration
in 1661 and, although the Earl of Winton had it
reprinted in 1712, it was little used after 1689. Instead
the English Book of Common Prayer became the
normal service book in episcopal meeting houses, to
the great enrichment of the Church. Its use was made
possible by one of the happy consequences of the Act of
Union of 1707. In Edinburgh the Rev. Mr. Greenshields
was imprisoned for using it. His appeal against

wrongous imprisonment was rejected by the Court of Session. The Union gave him the right to appeal to the House of Lords, where, in 1711, his appeal was successful, the Lords ruling that it could not be illegal to use in one part of Queen Anne's realm a book which was prescribed in the other part. The way was clear for all congregations to use it, as most continued to do so until the publication of a new Scottish liturgy in 1764. Well–wishers in England were generous in supplying copies of the prayer–book to Scottish congregations.

In St. Andrews there was to be a great financial encouragement to the incumbent to use the English book – the Anderson bequest. Dr. John Anderson, who had made a considerable fortune in the West Indies, left part of it to trustees requiring them to pay £10 sterling annually to the minister of the gospel in St. Andrews who performed divine service according to the liturgy of the Church of England. In the other university towns the trustees were to select one from among the episcopal clergy for this bounty. The first payment was made in 1742 and payments continued till the end of last century. The £10 so paid was a very considerable sum in the 18th century. The use of the English prayer book was not incompatible with Jacobite principles. A Jacobite officiant simply omitted the prayers for the royal family.

When Dr. Waddell prayed for Queen Anne and the house of Hanover he gave clear indication that he, if not all his congregation, had come to accept the new order. He had taken advantage of the Toleration Act of 1712, "An act to prevent the disturbing of those of the Episcopal Communion in that part of Great Britain

13

called Scotland, in the exercise of their religious worship, and in the use of the liturgy of the Church of England". The clergy protected by the act were those who took and subscribed the oaths of allegiance to Queen Anne and of abjuration of Rome and were prepared to pray publicly for the queen, the princess Sophia of Hanover and all the royal family. The act also gave such clergy the right to celebrate marriages and to baptise, rights of which they had been deprived by an act of the Scots parliament in 1695. Under the protection of the act the congregation was free for a time to worship publicly and escaped the effects of the harsh penal laws imposed on non–jurant clergy and people after the failure of the 1715 rising, when non–jurant episcopacy and Jacobitism were treated as synonomous terms by the government.

No record survives of the names of the first congregation. A few scattered references alone make it possible to see who the people were who joined in the worship of the meeting house. The university was strongly Jacobite, so strongly that a bullying parliamentary commission under the Earl of Crawford in 1690 saw to it that almost all the regents were deprived of their offices as disaffected persons. The students were also disaffected. They kept the 29th May, the date of the restoration of Charles II, as a holiday. Even worse in the eyes of the government they "did frequentlie molest and disturbe those of the presbyterian persuasione during the tyme of publict worshipe". The regents did little to discourage them. "Moreover these few Sabbaths past the Maisters have kept back their schollars from comeing to the Towne Church, becaus ministers of the presbyterian persuassion are preachers ther". Even after the disaffected regents were dismissed students continued to attend the episcopal meeting house. In 1705 the regents gave a testimonial in its favour.

"We the Regents in the University of St. Andrews ..... find ourselves obliged to declare that we have found no trouble or disturbance to our students by that meeting excepting that some of them, by their parents' order and authority frequent the same. Moreover we have good ground to believe that the singular methods taken here to shut up this meeting while meeting houses are connived at in other university seats within the kingdom leads very much to the desolation of our philosophie Colleges being that already upon the rumour of measures taken here several students of the best quality have deserted our university and gone elsewhere and others have altered their resolution of coming".[4]

The words "best quality" probably refer to social rather than academic standing. The testimonial was of no avail. In 1706 the meeting house was temporarily closed.

A letter to Robert Wodrow from William Dunlop, who was later to be professor of Church History in the University of Edinburgh gives a glimpse of Dr. Waddell's congregation in 1713:

"The congregation in this country are generally poisioned with ill principles which much

15

appear from their sons attending the Episcopal meeting–house in this place ..... for I believe the large half of students in both colleges go there ..... and a great many people in town are tainted with jacobitish principles, and the students fired guns throughout all the pretender's birthday, and I believe the imposter's health was generally drunk on that occasion, and though both the town and college churches are pretty throng, yet the archdeacon has by far the gentilest congregation in town".

Diocesan records are of no help in filling out the picture. The last episcopal archbishop of St.Andrews, Archbishop Ross died in 1704. In the absence of King James, who alone could issue a coge d'elire, no new appointment was made. Instead the oversight of the archdiocese was taken over by the Bishop of Edinburgh, Bishop Rose. There were no temporalities for this or any other diocese, for when the office of bishop was abolished by parliament in 1689 their revenues, the "bishops' rents" were taken into the national treasury. Bishop Rose could do no more than exercise a benevolent oversight of his vast spiritual domain and ordain to the priesthood such suitable men as sought orders. (It is said that he refused ordination to any who refused to swear loyalty to King James.) A more workable arrangement was made in 1743 when Robert White, the presbyter of Cupar, was made bishop of the new diocese of Fife. (He filled that office till his death in 1761, to be succeeded by Bishop Edgar. On Edgar's death in 1765 the separate diocese of Fife ceased to exist.)

The position of the bishops was an odd one. Prelacy

had been abolished in 1689, yet in 1704 a royal warrant ordered the Lords Commissioners of the Treasury "to order payment out of the first and readiest of Bishops' Rents in Scotland, of one hundred pounds sterling to each of these four Bishops following viz: to the Bishop of Edinburgh, the Bishop of Aberdeen, the Bishopi of Moray and to the Bishop of Dunblane". These payments were repeated in 1706. It is strange to find the office of bishop so recognised by the crown after parliament had abolished it. For the rest of the century and longer bishops were dependent on private means or on their stipends as ministers of congregations, which might be far removed from their diocese. Bishop Forbes, for example, combined the office of incumbent of Leith and Bishop of Ross and Caithness while the incumbent of Pittenweem, Bishop Low, for a time was Bishop of Ross, Argyll and Moray.

CHAPTER 2

Dr. Waddell was succeeded by James Morice though it is not clear whether Morice began to officiate immediately after Dr.Waddell's death or whether there was a short inter–regnum. Morice came to St. Andrews originally as tutor to the sons of Mackenzie of Delvine. He appears to have been a man of some substance for it needed eleven horses to transport his plenishings and books when he moved here and as early as 1716 he was able to lend money.[5] He married Cecilia, the daughter of Robert White, the incumbent of Cupar who later became Bishop of Fife. Morice died in 1739(?) Apart from these scanty facts little can be found out about him.

Happily more is known about the congregation during his incumbency. An English traveller in Scotland, John Loveday, finding himself in St. Andrews on Sunday August 13th 1732, made his way to the meeting–house and left this description of the service and congregation.

"We were at the Meeting–house on Sunday: 'tis a very ordinary Room indeed, not pew'd. The Minister read the Communion Service at a little table by the Pulpit, where, after some time, were placed the Collections made for the poor. So in the Kirk, part of the Deacons Office is to collect the offerings for the Poor at the Kirk–Doors, which is the only way in Scotland for providing of the Poor. The Person that stood at the Meeting–house door was Mr. Sharp, brother of Sir James Sharp, Bart., both Grandsons of the Archbishop, In the Afternoon after 'O God the Creator and preserver etc', followed a long prayer for the afflicted Church of Scotland, with several of the Collects at the end of the Communion Office".[6]

Where the meeting took place is not known. Oliphant surmises that it may have been in the house on the south side of South St to which reference is made later. Certainly there was no hint in the extract quoted that there was anything secret about the place or the time of the service. The author said nothing about the size of the congregation but the word "pulpit" implies that there were a respectable number of worshippers present. The penal laws of 1719 made it an offence for more than nine people, apart from the officiant's family, to be present at a service conducted by a clergyman who had not taken the oaths of loyalty and abjuration and did not pray for King George by name. We can infer that Mr. Morice had followed Dr. Waddell's practice and conformed. Oliphant in a footnote summarises an interesting article in the Proceedings of the Society of Antiquaries of Scotland of 1894 showing that the Mr. Sharp who stood at the door was probably the Alexander Sharp who won the university archery medal in 1710 and 1714. The descendants of the Archbishop were long in and round St. Andrews. Dr. Johnson in 1773 met at supper a Miss Sharp, the great grand daughter of the archbishop and in 1771 Alexander Sharp, son of Sir William Sharp was baptised. The family held the estate of Strathtyrum.

The most valuable documents for the 18th century congregation survived by chance. The first of these records baptisms from 1722 to 1740, with a gap from 1732 to 1734, 166 in number. The second part, which includes marriages as well as baptisms, covers the period from 1748 to 1787. 14 marriages and 191 baptisms are recorded in it. The story of the discovery and recovery is best told by Oliphant:

"They were found by Mr. George Cruickshank, postmaster of St. Andrews and a member of the vestry of the congregation from 1821 until shortly before his death in 1874, in a tobacconist's shop, where parts of them had already been used for wrapping up snuff. This must have been prior to 1843, as passing mention is made of these registers in Lyon's history which was published in that year".

Canon Winter edited them for the Scottish Record Society in 1916.

Of the names listed Oliphant said:

"The names in both parts of the registers are

nearly all Scottish, thus showing that the members of the congregation were not alien importations from England, and that the faith which they had received from their forefathers was no exotic as has often been falsely alleged in later days".

A glance at the index of names proves the truth of his statement, for the index of the register of births begins "Aitken, Aiton, Anderson, Arnot, Auchterlonie", and that for the register of marriages, "Douglas, Haliburton, Law, Lindsay, Melville, Neish, Norrie". There were exceptions. These are mainly the names of soldiers whose children were brought for baptism, men serving in the regiments which were stationed in the neighbourhood during the years covered by the registers as a defence against a possible Jacobite incursion from the north or French landings on the coast. The soldiers appear to have been well–conducted. Only two are cited as fathers of bastards, both of them Scots, one a soldier in the Sutherland Fencibles, the other the son of Principal Gillespie. Indeed the number of illegitimate children brought for baptism is surprisingly small, by the standard of the times, and not all the parents may have been members of the congregation, for it was common practice at the time to bring illegitimate children to the episcopal clergy for baptism to avoid the censure which the parents would receive in the established church.

It is significant that baptisms as well as marriages took place not in the meeting–house in the presence of the congregation but in the house of the parents. They usually took place on the day of birth or very shortly afterwards, a comment, perhaps, on the infants' expectation of life. Here in St. Andrews there appears to have been no need for baptisms ever to take place clandestinely. The registers contain no entries such as that found in the Muthill registers in 1750: "With such severity were the penal laws executed at this time ..... that we could not take the child into a house but I was obliged to go under the cover of Trees ..... to baptise the child."[7] It appears that the St. Andrews congregation enjoyed an unusual degree of toleration. To the penal laws and the question of toleration we will return later.

In one way these registers are disappointing: they tell us little about the occupations and social standing of the members of the congregation. We find a basket–maker from Kemback, a sailor, a wright, a lint–dresser, a convener of the trades and a few others but there are not enough of such entries to enable us to form a just opinion of the social composition of the congregation. By chance the volume of the "Scottish Records Society" which contains our registers also contains the register for the remote parish of Durness, a register which shows how informative such a document can be. There are to be found not only the English names but also the Gaelic patronymics and occupations of the parishioners. "James Munro alias Macmhorachie Macdholicorachie weaver in Erriboll" who married "Janet Mackay alias Nin Hustian", will serve as an example. The Durness register gives a picture of the economic and social life of the parish in the late 18th century, and we are left to regret that Mr. Morice and his successor did not add one word to each entry in their register.

If our registers tell little about townsfolk they are useful in showing how many of the local lairds adhered to episcopacy. Corstorphine of Nydie, Carstairs of Radernie, Arnot of Balkeathly, Erskine of Cambo, Lindsay of Feddinch, Robertson of Dunork, Bethune of Blebo, Wemyss of Lathocar, Martine of Clermont, Sibbald of Kinkell, Falconer of Balmashanner and Sir William Sharp all appear as parents or god–parents. Even Halkerston of Rathillet, the descendant of one of the murderers of Archbishop Sharp, figures as a god–father. It was a scattered congregation. Baptism took place as far afield as Earlshall and the now vanished castle of Leuchars. The fact that so many of the lairds were members was not without importance, for they gave standing and respectability to the church and their houses may have been places where services could be held during the few years when the penal laws appear to have been enforced in St. Andrews.

Another document surviving from the 18th century gives a list of the subscribers to the clergy and expenses of the services. We must assume that these sums were additional to whatever stipend was paid by the heads of families, for many of those paying were ladies of the congregation and some were well–wishers from out–with the area. The total amount paid each year was small. In 1769 for example the total, including a generous £25.4/–

23

from Halkerston of Rathillet but excluding the Anderson bequest, was £63 in Scots money, five guineas in sterling.

Even with this supplement to whatever small stipend the incumbent received he was not rich. Dr. Hay Fleming tells a story he had from an old man in the town about Mr. Robb who was incumbent at the end of the 18th century. He was asked by one of the parish ministers how he managed to make ends meet with his small stipend when the questioner had enough to do with his large one. Mr. Robb replied that it was just with them as with the Israelites in the wilderness. He who gathered much manna had nothing over, and he who gathered little had no lack.

Mr. Morice was succeeded by Mr. David Lindsay, a cadet of the house of Lindsay of Glenquoich, a family noted for its Jacobite and episcopal fervour. The exact date of his assuming the incumbency is uncertain, but certainly he had done so before 1742 when the Anderson bequest was paid to him. His ministry was a long one, almost half a century in length, for he died in office in 1791. It was a long one and a troubled one in his early years, which coincided with the great rising of 1745 and 1746.

In the years between 1720 and 1745 when the highlands were being opened up by roads and pacified in part by garrisons, Jacobites had lain low and episcopalians became less suspect. The severity of the penal law of 1719 was relaxed in practice if not in words. The rising of 1745 destroyed the toleration which the church had enjoyed. Episcopal meeting–houses were regarded by a frightened government as breeding grounds of Jacobitism. Cumberland's army on the way north closed, destroyed or vandalised meeting–houses and the residences of the clergy. A series of laws designed to curb, indeed to destroy the episcopal church in Scotland was enacted. By the first of these, "An act more effectually to prohibit and prevent pastors or ministers from officiating in Episcopal meeting–houses in Scotland, without duly qualifying themselves according to the law; and to punish persons for resorting to any meeting–house where such unqualified pastors or ministers shall officiate", was passed in the summer of 1746 soon after the butchery of Culloden. Clergy who did not take the oaths of allegiance and abjuration and pray for King George and the royal family by name were forbidden to conduct services attended by more than four people, other than members of the family living in the house. The penalties were heavy. For a first offence clergy were liable to imprisonment for six months; for any subsequent offence they were liable to transportation to the colonies for life. The laity were also subject to penalties for attending illegal services, suffering a fine of £5 for the first offence and the risk of two years imprisonment for a subsequent offence. Other disabilities, too numerous to list here, were also imposed. To ensure obedience to the law, rewards were offered to informers.

The second major penal law of that time was passed in 1748, an act plainly designed to extirpate native episcopacy. By this law no clergyman of the episcopal church, however loyal he might be, however ready to swear allegiance to and pray for King George, might officiate in the presence of more than four people, excluding the family, unless he had been ordained by a bishop of the church of England or Ireland. To the credit of the English clergy most of the bishops opposed the bill in the House of Lords, but without avail. The act not only deprived the existing clergy loyal to the house of Hanover of any right to conduct public services openly but effectively prevented young men from entering the ministry, for an English bishop could not ordain anyone who lacked some title to a church office in England by which he could support himself after ordination. Robert Southey gives an interesting account of the difficulties of one St. Andrews man, Andrew Bell, in seeking ordination in England even with influential support. The full story can be found in Southey's "Life" of Dr. Andrew Bell.

The effect of such legislation on the worship of the church was grave. For a time various ways of circumventing the laws were used. Non–jurant clergy conducted services in private houses with the right number of people present in the room and the door or window left open so that those gathered in an adjoining room or outside might share in the service. Sometimes the clergy conducted services in several houses on the same day. Such services tended to be very quiet gatherings. Bishop Forbes in Leith tells how after a visit from a party of dragoons he decided that no singing should take place in

26

future. George Grub in his "Ecclesiastical History of Scotland" sums up one consequence of the laws:

"The persecution which destroyed the meeting–houses almost extinguished the solemnities of religious worship; and both clergy and people became so accustomed to irregularities, that, on the return of tranquillity, they hardly made an effort to remove them".

In St. Andrews, however well people might be disposed to episcopalians as friends and neighbours, the law could not be disregarded at first. Hay Fleming notes a tradition that, though the St. Andrews meeting–house was not burned, probably from fear of setting fire to adjoining property, the contents of the building, the altar and furnishings, were dragged into the street and burned. The action may have been no more than that of a drunken mob confident that, in the climate of opinion of the time, no penalty would ensue. (There is a legend that one of the mob who burned the communion table was shortly afterwards paralysed in both hands.) More serious was the enforced closure of the meeting–house in November 1746 when Margaret Skinner, the widow of David Rankeillour, a merchant in St. Andrews, who had allowed a room in her house to be used as the meeting–house, undertook not to do so.

"Whereas by the late Act of Parliament ..... it is ordained that all the aforesaid Meeting–houses shall be shut up by the Civil Magistrate and no access be again given to the said houses until the proprietor enact him or herself under the penalty of one hundred pounds sterling, that such house shall not be employed as a Meeting–house in time coming: And whereas there is a house belonging to me in liferent, lying on the south side of South St of St. Andrews, which was lately employed as a meeting–house by a non–jurant Episcopal Minister and those of the communion. Therefore, in obedience to the foresaid Act of Parliament, I hereby bind me, my heirs, executors and successors, that the foresaid House, belonging to me in liferent, shall not in time coming be set (i.e. let) by me, nor shall I permit the same to be used and employed by any person or persons of the Episcopal Communion, non–jurant".

For a time thereafter the congregation cannot have met as a congregation. We must presume that here as elsewhere small groups of the faithful gathered in one another's houses to worship in secret. But toleration returned and although the laws remained in force till 1792 they seem to have been ignored here. Mrs. Berkeley, the wife of a canon of Canterbury, who lived in St. Andrews in the 1780s, wrote: "To the honour of the Editor's presbyterian neighbours in St. Andrews she never saw the Episcopalians incommoded though they assembled in much larger numbers at Mr. Lindsay's chapel" (i.e. in much larger numbers than the law permitted).[8] In 1773 when Dr. Johnson visited the town Boswell noted:

"We saw in one of the streets a remarkable proof of liberal toleration: a non–juring clergyman strutting about in his canonicals with a jolly countenance and a round belly like a well–fed monk."[9]

Once congregational worship could resume again a meeting place was found in a house now demolished. Oliphant learned, at second hand admittedly, that the episcopalians met in "Tam Couper's big room" in a house on the site of the present Town Hall. He tells, too of a later meeting place, "St. Leonard's Hall – the large upper room still to be seen in the old part of St. Leonards School." In a service there, his informant told him, something occurred which illustrates plainly how in the troubled times seemliness of service had been lost. "The sermon was long, and may have been dry; the minister certainly was, as he suddenly startled the congregation by calling to his servant to bring him a bottle of ale; 'and mind, Betty' he added, 'that it's well corked'. The ale having been produced and consumed, Mr. Robb – it was he who was then the minister – continued his discourse". the story illustrates clearly George Grub's statement.

CHAPTER 3

The death of the "Young Pretender", King Charles III to loyal Jacobites, in 1788 made it possible for the Church to accept George III as rightful king and so to free itself from most of the restraints imposed by the Penal Laws. The bishops met in the same year in Aberdeen when all, except the Bishop of Edinburgh who was in his dotage, agreed to petition parliament to repeal the Penal Laws and to urge the clergy to pray for King George. The vast majority of the clergy complied with the advice though a few, such as Donald MacIntosh, the collector of Gaelic proverbs, held out. A few of the laity also held out. Oliphant of Gask for example forbade the incumbent of Muthill to enter his house after he began praying for King George.

The petition to parliament, supported as it was both by the English bishops and by the leaders of the established Church of Scotland, was successful, leading to "An Act for granting relief to Pastors, Ministers and Lay Persons of the Episcopal Communion in Scotland" of 1792. The act did not remove all the disabilities imposed earlier, but it did remove the most grievous of them, particularly the restriction of the size of the congregation and the requirement that clergy should be ordained by bishops of the English or Irish Church. The remaining disabilities were gradually removed during the next two centuries, though some lingered long. It was not till 1948 that non-jurant episcopalians were free to vote in parliamentary elections, nor were they permitted to hold services behind locked doors till 1977. It is, of course, possible that some long-forgotten piece of anti-episcopalian legislation may still lurk in the statute book. The way was now clear for congregations to assemble legally in any number and to hold property as a corporate body.

Mr. William Robb, who became presbyter in 1791 when Mr. Lindsay died, obviously accepted and welcomed the bishops' decision, expressing his opinions in verse soon after he assumed the charge. His "Patriotic Wolves, a Fable by a Scotch Episcopalian Clergyman" of 1793 was an elegant little fable designed to warn its readers against attempts to subvert the constitution. The opening lines, addressed to Britannia, run:

"Long may the monarch wear the crown!
His foes be to destruction hurl'd!
Long may'st thou flourish in renown
The dread and envy of the world".10

It is a far cry from Bishop Robert Forbes' toast: "The Scotch thistle. May the white horse choke on it", a white horse being part of the arms of the House of Hanover.

During Mr. Robb's ministry the congregation met in several different houses. St. Leonard's hall has already been mentioned. Oliphant states that in 1804 Mr. Robb bought Queen Mary's house, erecting an outside stair to give access to a chapel on the first floor. This house was sold in 1821. For a time the congregation met in "Priorsgate" before moving to the upper room of a house in North Street, conveniently provided with an outside stair. "As far as can be ascertained it was where the house number 5 North Street now stands – one of those occupied by the men of H.M. Coastguard", to quote Oliphant. It was the last temporary home of the congregation.

Mr.Robb left St. Andrews in 1818 but apparently retained the incumbency till 1820. In his place a Mr. Bailey served for a time to be followed in 1821 by Mr. Robert Young, the assistant to the incumbent in Cupar. During his ministry the congregation acquired a constitution and a church. On July 11th 1821 "a meeting of the Scotch Episcopal Chapel took place in consequence of intimation being duly given by the officiating clergyman on the Sunday preceding. present:– Dr. Thomas Melville, Mrs. Lambert, Miss Fowlis, Miss Graham and others". At this meeting it was decided to appoint a vestry to manage the affairs of the congregation, a decision immediately acted upon. Alexander Binny Esq. Dr. Thomas Melville, Major William Holcroft, Mr. George Cruikshank, Colonel Robert Moodie and the Reverend Robert Young formed the first vestry. There now existed a corporate body which could hold property. It is noteworthy that in 1821 women members of the congregation had a say in the election of the vestry, for this right was not restored till the constitution of 1890 came into force.

The new vestry lost no time. In 1823 a firm decision was taken to build a church, to open a subscription list and to ask the bishop to solicit help from the English bishops. They also asked the Town Council for a piece of land at the east end of North Street. When this request was not granted they were able in 1824 to obtain from a Captain Mason a different piece of ground in North Street on which to build, ground which is now occupied by the east part of "College Gate". Everything was done at speed. On July 12th the decision was taken to acquire the ground. On August 24th contracts with tradesmen were signed. On August 27th the foundation stone was laid with great Masonic pomp. On 29th September 1825 the completed church was consecrated, by Bishop Low of Pittenweem under letters dimissory from the Bishop of Edinburgh, and dedicated to St. Andrew. Little more than a year elapsed between the decision to build and the completion of the building by men whose materials had to be brought to the site by horse and cart, and whose business had to be conducted by hand–written letters. The architect was William Burn, who was later to be the architect of the Madras College. The total cost, £1486.17.8?, a huge sum, for a congregation which in the 1820s seldom had an income of more than £90. The money for the new church came in part from members of the congregation, in part from wellwishers in Scotland and England and from India, where £86 was raised. The most munificent of the well–wishers was Dr. Andrew Bell who gave £300, following up this munificence by bequeathing £500 and his communion plate to the church. Others were also generous. By the time the church was completed £1200 had been subscribed. Some of the subscribers were slow to pay. One English Cathedral Chapter paid in 1991 after a reminder from the rector. By 1834 all was paid for and sufficient money remained to present Mr. Cruickshank, who had acted as treasurer, with a silver tea service.

Because of the shape of the ground which the vestry had acquired the main axis of the church had to be from north to south, with two short transepts running east and west. The overall length was sixty two feet with a thirty foot wide nave and a width across the transepts of fifty two feet. The Ordnance Survey map of 1855 shows very clearly the plan and the situation of the church.

Internally there was little architectural richness or ornamentation. The walls were painted grey with lines to represent ashlar. The nave and transepts were filled with pews of red pine painted to resemble oak, providing seating for two hundred worshippers, including the Whyte–Melville family who alone enjoyed the privilege of a double pew, seated all round, with a table in the middle. (They sacrificed it after a while to make room for a growing congregation). There was a pulpit and reading desk of oak and an altar covered with red

Utrecht velvet cloth behind which two doors led into a small vestry. A sentence of Oliphant's throws a little light on the practice of the 1830s. "In Mr. Lyon's time, when it was still the custom to wear a black gown for preaching, he used to enter the vestry by the door nearest the reading desk and, having effected the change of raiment dictated by the ritual of the period, he came out by the other and ascended the pulpit". This pulpit was transferred to the present church where it continued to be used until 1889 when some ladies of the congregation presented the pulpit now in use.

At first there was neither organ nor font. For lack of evidence we may assume that in earlier times the singing was either led by a precentor or, possibly, accompanied by the music of a barrel organ. A real organ came in 1833 through the generosity of Mr. Alexander Binny, a scandal no doubt to strict presbyterians in the town. It was placed at the end of the east transept on a raised platform to which access was gained for the organist and small choir through the east window, converted for the purpose into a glass door. The first organist was a Miss Cowan who was given an honorarium of five guineas for the year's work. She was followed by a Miss Rackstraw, and she in turn by Mr. Salter who was to remain an organist till 1871. (The lectern and a window on the south aisle of the present church commemorate him.) The church and the town owe much to him, for not only did he begin to build the musical tradition of the church but also by his work as a private teacher

35

and by his enthusiastic teaching of "sacred music" to pupils of the Madras College, he began the regeneration of church music in the town.

There is some doubt about the composition of the early choir which sat in front of the organ behind a curtain. To begin with it was a mixed choir, for in 1838 £2.8/– was disbursed as payment to four girls and two boys in the choir. At some time soon afterwards the use of girls' voices ceased and the choir became, and long remained, a choir of men and boys. The role of the choir at first was confined to leading the praise. The responses were the responsibility of a succession of clerks beginning with a James Teviotdale in 1836 and ending in 1856 with Elias Jones.

It took some time for the practice of baptism in church rather than at home to become established. When it first took place baptism, for lack of a font, doubtless took place in "a decent bason to be provided by the Parish" as the Prayer Book has it. A font came as a gift from the widow of the Reverend James Justus Turner, a chaplain in the service of the Honourable East India Company. It was copied from the font in Trumpington parish church and was placed in church in 1846, sited, oddly, a few feet in front of the centre of the altar rails. This font, too, was transferred to the present church where it was raised in height by erecting it on a plinth.

The income of the church was not large at first. In 1827 it was no more than £75 but the hope was expressed that "by the addition of some families an annual produce may be looked for of about £100." Even with his £10 from the Anderson bequest Mr. Young must have lived sparingly. The hope of increase was fulfilled. During the sixteen years from 1833 to 1848 the average income rose to £121, an income drawn partly from collections which averaged £38 and mainly from pew rents yielding £83. Until 1861 when pew–by–pew collection began collections were taken in a plate at the door under the watchful eye of a member of the vestry. Pew rents which were from the beginning the main source of income, were a great convenience to the treasurer and an annoyance to many members of the congregation. They provided the treasurer with a regular income, which was relatively easy to collect but they drew a sharp line between the poor and the rest of the congregation. The system worked in this way. Heads of families rented as many sittings in church as their family required, usually in pews of their choice. Once they had paid their rent they regarded the seats as property over which they exercised tenants' rights, insisting often on the places remaining vacant even when few of the family were present, and handing them over, almost sub–letting them, in their absence to the summer holiday–makers who rented their houses. For those too poor to pay, seats were reserved in a section of the church – behind the font in the present church. The treasurer with the consent of the vestry was allowed some discretion in the rates he charged. He could temper the wind to the shorn lambs, and permit employers to pay a reduced rate for seats to be occupied by their domestic servants. This system of financing the church remained in use till 1963 when the vestry agreed to end it.

Mr. Young resigned in 1832 at the request of the vestry, with the support of the bishop, "The causes are not explicitly stated, and there is no need at this distance of time to enquire too closely into them", as Oliphant tactfully put it. He was succeeded by a man admirably suited to the congregation and the climate of the time, Charles J. Lyon. Mr. Lyon was of gentle birth, a younger son of the house of Lyon of Glen Ogil, educated at Trinity College, Cambridge and a former army chaplain. His position in St. Andrews society was assured by private means, by connection by marriage to the Playfair family and by his scholarly "History of St. Andrews", a work from which all later writers have drawn heavily. His work as incumbent is best summed up in the words of Oliphant "Judging from the evidence of many still living who remember him, as well as from the written records which are left to us, it was a time of steady, earnest, quiet work by a faithful and beloved priest among a happy and contented people". His incumbency lasted till 1854 when ill health compelled him to retire.

The years of his ministry were years of steady growth in the size of the congregation and in the size of the population of the town, which grew from about 3000 at the beginning of the 19th century to a little less than 7000 at the end of it. By 1845 there were in the congregation 32 families comprising 185 members, 20 boarders in the town, 6 students and 8 domestic servants, a total of 169 souls. By 1853 numbers had so increased that it was found necessary to enlarge the church by prolonging the nave southward to the limit of the site on North Street. The gable facing the street was built to a design of Sir Gilbert Scott, "a very rich Gothic structure, finer than any modern building in our city" as the "Fife Herald" of the time described it. The wealth of the congregation had also increased. The extension which cost almost £450 was paid for out of funds in the hands of the vestry, supplemented by the proceeds of a "Fancy Fair" in the Town Hallorganised by the ladies of the congregation, who employed one of the ubiquitous German bands to enliven their market.

Newspaper reports of the fair and of a fair held a week later by the ladies of the United Presbyterian church suggest that the episcopal community was still a closed one. The episcopal fair, in spite of the band, attracted no more than two hundred or so visitors, mainly members of the congregation and their friends, and produced about £90. the United Presbyterian one, which produced £154 was attended by some 800 people. The "Fife Herald" was sharp in its comment, regretting that "a wealthier ecclesiastical body" should steal a march on the United Presbyterians by holding its fair a week before the other.

There were twelve confirmations during Mr. Lyon's incumbency, seven of them conducted by Bishop Low of Moray, Ross and Argyll, the incumbent of Pittenweem, in the absence of the elderly Bishop Torry, the diocesan, who was incumbent of Peterhead. In all 137 people were confirmed, 85 men and 52 women.

The growth of the episcopal congregation was matched by equal or greater growth in other congregations, especially after the Disruption in the established church in 1843. By 1839 it was found necessary to build St. Mary's Church, the building which is now the Victory Memorial Hall, as an extension to Holy Trinity. In the next thirty years the Baptist Church, Martyrs' Church, the Congregational Church, which stood until recently in Bell Street, and Hope Park Church were all built or enlarged. The new buildings symbolised more than the increasing size of the town and wealth of its inhabitants. They symbolised the spiritual quickening of the mid–century which had such profound effects not only on the religious and moral life of the community but also on a much wider world. From these congregations were to come finance and help for missionary work overseas and for church extension work in the growing industrial towns. As early as 1836, to take one example from many, the little episcopal congregation here sent £5 to help build a chapel for the poor Irish episcopalians in Glasgow, a token of the caring attitude for others which continued and increased as the years went by.

Mr. Lyon's successor was an exemplar of the new caring outlook. He was the Reverend Henry Macnamara, a member of an Irish family, the Macnamaras of Rathfolen in County Nore, an Oxford graduate who had served as a curate in Deptford. His stay in St. Andrews was brief, no more than two years, and his reason for leaving interesting, for he left because he found that there was not enough work for an energetic priest and, especially, hardly any among the poor. His short incumbency saw one change in the calendar of services: on October first 1854 the first recorded Harvest Festival was held, the collection on that day going to "the relief of families left destitute by the ravages of cholera." From St. Andrews he moved to Dundee where he remained, with a short break, for the rest of his life, working with the saintly Bishop Forbes, serving the people of the overcrowded tenements – native episcopalians, members of the Church of Ireland who had fled the famine in Ireland, converts from other denominations and those of none. Work among the poor he had then in plenty providing the comfort of the services to the living, cholera medicine to the sick, soup to the hungry and the sacraments to the dying.

CHAPTER 4

When Mr. Macnamara left, the incumbency was offered to the Reverend Robert Skinner, an Edinburgh man, who had trained as a priest in Durham. He came from a family reverenced in the Church, for he could claim kinship with two former Skinner bishops of Aberdeen and with Dean Skinner of Dunkeld, and boast that he was the great–grand–nephew of the Reverend John Skinner of Longside, "Tullochgorm" the poet, who had suffered imprisonment under the Penal Laws. The new incumbent was instituted in the summer of 1856 after an extraordinary hitch. The vestry had obviously not read the constitution of 1825 which required the incumbent to be "a person invested with orders by the Episcopal Church of Scotland" otherwise they could not have accepted either Mr. Lyon or Mr. Macnamara. Mr. Skinner's institution had to wait until episcopal sanction was given to abrogate the clause which required Scottish ordination, for he, like them, had been ordained in England.

The new ministry was to be one of great achievement and of petty squabbles, a time when the present church was built and when the vestry and the incumbent were often at loggerheads. The old vestry and the new one which was elected in 1862 were composed of men of a conservative cast of mind, men who were content with the existing services, suspicious of changes in the forms of worship, reluctant to enlarge the congregation by hasty evangelism, decorous in their public behaviour and, above all, convinced that they had authority over everything connected with the church – Sir Charles Ochterlony, General Moncrieff, Colonel Mackay, Colonel Hunter, Mr. Whyte–Melville, Principal Forbes and others. The new incumbent had plainly brought with him some of the new ideas which underlay the ferment in the Church of England, especially the view that the forms of public worship should be enriched by restoring some of the practices which had been abandoned at the Reformation. He brought, too, the view that the Church should be more outward–looking, should interest itself more in the well–being of the poor, and should be a missionary force in the community.

The ideas were not new in Scotland. The work of Bishop Forbes in Dundee was a shining example of church involvement in the social and economic as well as the spiritual life of the town. Reform in the worship of the church had been hastened by the increasing number of incumbents from England who served the increasing number of congregations formed in the mid–century. When Bishop Torry held a diocesan synod in St. Andrews in 1838 there were no more than nine charges in the huge diocese

– five in Dunkeld, one in Dunblane, and three in Fife. Yet by 1854 there were twenty three charges. Like expansion was taking place in other dioceses. To fill the charges it was necessary, for lack of sufficient native priests, to invite English clergy to come to Scotland. Many who came were strongly influenced by the ritualistic side of the Oxford Movement, extravagantly so sometimes, introducing ornaments, elaborate vestments and ritual into their churches to the dismay of older episcopalians who were accustomed to a church which was high in doctrine but low in practice. These men acted as a leaven in the worship of the Church.

The disputes between the vestry and Mr. Skinner began early and lasted throughout his incumbency. By 1863 he was writing to the clerk, "As vestry matters have long been a constant source of vexation to my mind, indeed so much as to impair my health, I have resolved to meddle no more with such matters". Happily he did not adhere to his resolve. Money difficulties occurred early in his ministry, for although the congregation contained a fair number of wealthy men their liberality did not match their wealth. In a letter in 1862 Mr. Skinner wrote to the vestry, "Gentlemen, As I find that my stipend together with my own resources is quite inadequate for the support of my family in this place I beg that the greatly improved state of the Congregational funds (which are likely to be even further increased) may induce you kindly to consider the necessity of augmenting my income from the church". His plea was attended to in small measure. The vestry agreed to relieve him of the burdens of external repairs to the parsonage at 1 Playfair Terrace, which had been bought in 1858, and of the £10 a year interest on the debt on the parsonage. They agreed also to allow him 1/3 of the surplus income of the church in addition to his stipend – an annual bonus dependent on his efforts. This unsatisfactory arrangement ended in 1868 when it was replaced by an increase of £45 a year.

Music was another source of discord. As early as 1856 Mr. Skinner tried to effect some improvement, or at least changes, in the music used in church and the vestry was asked by a member of the congregation to give a ruling "regarding the right of the incumbent to direct and control the music and singing of the church". (Perhaps the organist's voice was raised). The vestry referred the problem to the bishop who gave a ruling which is worth quoting in full for it was of great help to Mr. Skinner's successors. "There can be no question that every incumbent ought to have entire control over the music and singing, as over every other part of the service performed in church". In spite of that ruling the vestry still resisted Mr. Skinner's freedom to innovate. "Hymns Ancient and Modern" was published in 1861 and enthusiastically welcomed by many who found it a treasury of hymns for all occasions. Mr. Skinner tried to introduce it soon after its publication as a means of replacing, or supplementing, the metrical psalms. The vestry objected vigorously and for a time the project had to be abandoned. Perhaps his interest in music was not always wisely directed. His good singing voice made him a welcome guest at concerts and banquets in the town where his renderings of some of the songs of "Tullochgorm" were very popular. There is nothing indecorous about these humorous songs, but it was unusual for a clergyman of the period to act as a public entertainer at banquets where the toast–lists were very lengthy indeed.

Further objections were made by the vestry to Mr. Skinner's attempts to widen the appeal of the church. Evensong at that time in St. Andrews, as in most other places, was at half–past two. It was a time which suited all who came from outlying places by carriage or gig or on foot, for it gave them time for lunch after morning service and daylight for their return journey in winter. To supplementevensong Mr. Skinner began to hold evening services of a popular nature, opening the church to domestics who had the evening off and to others who were reluctant to attend regular services or unwilling (or unable) to pay a pew rent. These irregular services were a source of grievance to some of the vestry who succeeded in having them abandoned, for a time. Similar objections were made to the Sunday School which Mr. Skinner started in a private home in South Street. He used there a new form of catechism, not the Prayer Book form, and was not too careful to ensure that all the children who attended were offspring of Episcopal parents. (Sunday School was popular at that time with both parents and children Non churchgoing parents salved their consciences by sending their children there. Children who had very few treats knew that the reward for regular attendance was the annual treat when unaccustomed cakes and buns came their way, when there might be a magic–lantern show, and even a present. It is said that some managed to attend more than one Sunday School.)

The final episode in this sad story came after the service at the opening of the new church. Mr. Skinner had ventured to dignify the service by inviting a surpliced choir from Edinburgh to take part, to the great indignation of some of the vestry who seemed to see in surplices the trappings of Rome.

The disharmony between incumbent and vestry over forms of worship did not interfere with the steady growth of the congregation. By 1865 the vestry had to consider extending the North Street church by widening the nave on the west side, going so far as to have plans for this prepared by John Milne, the architect for the enlargement of Martyr's church. In the end it was decided that a new church should be built in the Scores, or in Howard Place or on a suitable site elsewhere. Bishop Wordsworth was asked to draft an appeal for funds, to be widely distributed. A building committee of Sir Charles Ochterlony, General Moncrieff, D.L. Burn (the brother of the architect of the old church) and Mr. Skinner was appointed and a search made for a site. The choice fell on the piece of ground at the south end of Queen Street, the present Queen's Gardens, which was being developed at that time. At first sight there was a real obstacle to using ground there as the site for a church. The feu charters of the

Outside the old church in North Street

proprietors in that street, charters granted by the Town Council as the feudal superior, forbade the erection of any building on the west side of the street without the consent of all the proprietors and the Town Council. It says much for the standing of the congregation and the ecumenical spirit of the proprietors and the Town Council that consent was given to waiving the terms of the charters and allowing the church to be built. To obtain the ground on the west side the vestry had also to take the feu on the east side, the ground now occupied by St. Regulus' Hall. Happily Mr. McGregor, the future provost whose portrait looks benignly down today on auction sales, relieved the vestry of the feu and allowed it to enlarge its site by granting a strip eight feet wide on the north side. His benevolence went further: he granted the vestry a servitude over the ground to the west of the present church, so making possible further extension of church building.

By June 1866 the site was secured. Two architects, the experienced John Milne and the young Robert Rowand Anderson were invited to submit plans. The plans were in the hands of the vestry by October when, on the advice of G.E.Street, an eminent architect of the period, the design of Rowand Anderson was chosen – a brave choice because Anderson was barely in his thirties at the time. His design was for the church we know today, to which, when funds permitted, a square tower topped by a lofty spire was to be added. It was a noble concept, a symbol of resurgent episcopacy to all who approached the town from the south. The congregation struggled hard, though unsuccessfully,

The proposed tower and spire for the "Cathedral", c.1870

over many years to bring it to completion. Some members had dreams of an enhanced status for it. The term "The Cathedral Church of St. Andrew" was used as if it was destined to be the episcopal seat of a bishopric of St. Andrews separated from Dunkeld and Dunblane. Bishop Wordsworth gave a very cautious assent to the use of the term saying, "The title is to be an honorary one, and not to interfere in any way with the status and privileges of St. Ninian's Perth, as at present the Cathedral of the United Diocese". The term was later abandoned, perhaps at the bishop's urging.

In April 1867 tenders for the building work were allocated:

Mason work	£2826	J. McIntosh
Slating	£ 130	D. Anderson
Joinery	£1215	J.R. Swan
Plaster work	£ 52	J.D. McPherson
Plumbing	£ 159	J. Hart

The foundation stone, under the north pier of the chancel, was laid on July 31st with full Masonic honours, by John Whyte–Melville, the Grand Master Mason of Scotland, in the presence of Bishop Wordsworth and a representative number of clergy and citizens. The ceremony wasfollowed by lunch in the Royal Hotel, the present Southgait, at a cost of £45.

The last full service in the old church was held on April 4th 1869. On the Thursday following, April 8th, the present church was used for the first time.

At quarter past eight the dedication service took place, to be followed by Matins at half past eleven and evensong at half past seven, the Bishop of Brechin preaching at Matins in place of the Primus, who was indisposed, and the Bishop of Edinburgh at Evensong. It should have been a triumphal day, but discord still flourished.

In his last sermon in the old church Mr. Skinner had preached on the rebellion of Korah, Dathan and Abiram, a sermon directed at the rebellions in his congregation. The sermon had little effect. Indeed it may have blown to flames smouldering embers for on April 7th a memorial was sent to the bishop by representatives, as they alleged, of eighty seat–holders asking to be allowed to retain the old church and form a separate congregation under an incumbent of their own choice. The memorialists complained of the changes Mr. Skinner was making in the services and how necessary it was that he should stop doing so to avoid a disruption which would have grievous effects on the finances of the new church. Their request was not granted but to give time for rancour to dissipate Mr. Skinner took six months leave of absence at the end of which he effected an exchange with the vicar of Lea Marston in Warwickshire, the Reverend Laurence Tuttiet, receiving from the vestry a supplement of £50 a year for five years to bring his English stipend up to his St. Andrews stipend. It was an unhappy end to a ministry in which so much had been accomplished and we can be glad that Mr. Skinner's later years in England and as chaplain in Berne, in Cologne and in Leipzig were happier ones.

CHAPTER 5

If press reports can be taken as fair representations of public opinion the new church was rather a disappointment to the St. Andrews public. Both the "Fife Herald" and the "Citizen" damned it with faint praise. The more charitable report in the "Citizen" reads:

"The opening of the New Episcopal Church took place on Thursday. The new church is a gothic structure. It has a plain arched roof of painted oak and stone pillars partly of red sandstone. The passages are laid with brick which gives the building rather a cold appearance almost bordering on discomfort. The great display of ornamentation is in the chancel and round the altar where the floor is laid with a finer texture of fancy bricks. The altar itself is beautifully carved. The acoustic properties of the church seem very good. Beyond this there is no remarkable feature in the building."

The vestry had no reason to apologise for the plainness of the interior. With the money they had in hand and what they hoped to raise they had built a church large enough for a congregation which, they could be sure, would grow as the town expanded. Ornament and furnishing would come later either from private benevolence or from congregational funds. For the moment plain pine–wood pews sufficed.

All refinements had to wait till the debt on the church was paid. For the next eight years all the financial energy of the congregation was devoted to this, in big ways and small ways. One of these small ways makes us realise that Victorian St. Andrews was not quite the idyllic place it seems in retrospect. When in April 1870 Professor Oakley gave an organ recital to raise money, admission was by ticket only "to prevent the Church being filled by a disorderly rable (sic)" as the vestry minutes record.

By November 1877 the debt had been paid. The sale of the old church[11] and of the parsonage, which Mr. Skinner's successor did not want to occupy, had yielded £1311; the Ladies Committee had raised £683; bazaars and sales of work had brought in £726; donations had added£675; and special collections, surplus revenue and a small balance in the ordinary funds had given the rest, leaving a surplus of eight shillings and eleven pence. In eight years then, the congregation had paid off a debt of more than £3,000.

The way was clear for the church to be dedicated by Bishop Wordsworth on St. Andrew's Day 1877 during a service which must have seemed unduly

Projected design of the interior of the new church.

ritualistic to old members of the congregation:

"At noon the procession entered by the south door headed by the choir of St. James' Church, Leith, chanting the twenty fourth psalm and slowly proceeded to the Chancel which barely sufficed to hold them and the great throng of clergy. The services were choral, being intoned by the Rev. Gilbert Jackson of St. James', Leith with the support of his choir".

A contemporary description of the decoration of the church for the ceremony throws light on the taste, and wealth, of the congregation:

"The gas standards were wreathed with flowers and evergreens and along the low wall ferns set in moss. At the base of the lectern was a bank of moss in which were bouquets of hot–house flowers and a saltire or St. Andrew's Cross of camellias and chrysanthemums. Each compartment of the pulpit was covered with a frame–work of moss and white camelias with a Latin cross of white chrysanthemums in the centre. The sills of the windows in both aisles were filled with hot–house flowers set in moss."

Once the debt of the church was paid the congregation enthusiastically began to raise the money necessary to build the tower and spire which the architect had planned, and to enrich the church internally. Bazaars, donations surplus revenue, and special offertories brought in £1892, a sum sufficient to build the tower but not the spire. By 1892 the tower was complete to a height of more than eighty feet, built of six hundred tons of stone from the same quarry at Strathkinness from which the stone for the church came. The upper chamber had louvred openings and brackets were built into the walls to support bells, but these were never provided either through lack of funds or because there were doubts about the legality of using bells. For the next forty six years the tower stood as one of the landmarks of the town, especially prominent to those who came by the Largo Road or made their journey from the Mount Melville railway station.

Gradually the interior of the church was enriched. In 1879 the architect was asked to prepare designs for carving the foliage on the capitals of the pillars and some of the other stonework in church. Much of the carving was done at the expense of individual members of the congregation. The choir raised £30 for this purpose through a concert and the rest of the cost was met by an opportune legacy. In 1881 Mrs. Salter the widow of Edmund Salter who was organist from 1847 to 1871, presented the brass lectern, a copy of the lectern in the episcopal church in Forfar, in memory of her husband. The reredos depicting the Ascension came in 1884. It was designed by Robert Speir of Culdees, a devout churchman, and executed by the firm of James Powell and Sons. In the same year Mr. Robert Curwen of Westerlee presented the altar rails and Mr. Oliphant gave a lenten cloth – the first of the sequence of canonical colours which was complete in 1893 when Mrs. Oliphant presented a white one and a group of the congregation a red one.

The Oliphants were benefactors of the church in other ways. Mrs. Oliphant was the leader and inspirer of the group of ladies who in 1894 provided the present pulpit with its figures of the evangelists carved by J.S. Gibson. A sad event prompted Mr. Oliphant to make another gift to the church. During the Boxer rising in China his son David, once a chorister, was killed in the defence of the British legation in Pekin. In his memory Mr. Oliphant presented the choir stalls, graceful examples of flamboyant gothic carving. The rails which separate chancel from nave, and the carved quatre foils in the wall below them were the gift in 1893 of Captain Dashwood Fowler, in whose memory his widow presented the chancel gates two years later. Two other pieces of furnishing in the chancel deserve notice. The 18th century brass basin in which alms are received at the altar was a gift from Captain Jackson who found it in an antique shop in Norway. (It came originally from the Lutheran church near Molde where it served as a baptismal vessel). On the north side of the chancel are placed the bishop's chair and staff presented to Bishop Wordsworth by the congregation shortly before his death in 1892. They were made of oak from Christ Church College Oxford, wood given for the purpose by the Dean, Dean Liddell, the father of Lewis Carrol's "Alice".

Not all the gifts offered were accepted. The suspicion of anything savouring of Rome, or of the practices of the "High" party in the church induced the vestry to decline some offers. An early offer of candlesticks and another of a jewelled altar cross were both declined. Two brass altar vases were accepted but at first conditions were attached to their use – they might be used at great festivals only.

Under the patient persistence of Mr. Tuttiett the forms of service settled into a pattern which survived, with one major change, till the 1970s. In this the influence of Bishop Wordsworth was great.

After he came to live in St. Andrews he was a regular worshipper in church where his advice, when offered, or sought, was heeded, both because of his office and because of the wisdom in human relations he had slowly acquired during his difficult years in Perth. It was he, for example, who persuaded the vestry that the money needed to add the spire could be better used to pay for a church hall. Oliphant quotes another example of how his influence was felt. Finding that some members of the choir refused to face east during the creed, the bishop wrote a tract on the subject and sent each member a copy. "Next Sunday one place was vacant, but all the members present turned to the east." He too, helped to overcome the prejudice which existed in part of the congregation against the wearing of surplices by the choir, a choir which grew in number and discipline during the 80s. In 1879 the vestry decided that there should be a choir of four men and ten or twelve boys, the men to be paid £5 a year and the boys £2, with deductions for absence from practices or services and extra payment for weddings and funerals. This choir was supplemented by volunteers, men and women until 1881 when the use of women singers ceased, for a time. In that year the number of boys was increased to sixteen and cassocks and surplices were provided for all.

From 1847 to 1871 the organist and choir master was Mr. Edmund Salter. After his resignation the post was held for short periods first by Mr. C. Campling, then by Mr. F. Turner, then by Miss Ada Boucher. When she resigned in 1878 the vestry had the good fortune to find and appoint Mr. Charles Freeman from Basingstoke. For the next fifty years he served the congregation and taught generation after generation of boys to use their voices in God's praise.

Under Mr. Tuttiett's guidance the congregation learned decorum in worship. The practice of coming late into church was stopped in 1881 when the annual general meeting resolved that the doors of the church should be closed as soon as the service began and not opened again until the Confession, Absolution and Lord's Prayer had been said. Two practices which we now accept as customary were gradually adopted – the practice of the congregation standing when the choir and clergy enter, and that of the congregation remaining standing till the choir and clergy have withdrawn. It took time for the older members of the congregation to accept these novelties, especially the second, for they had been used to rush out the moment the final "amen" had been said.

By the time Mr. Tuttiett retired the form of worship in church was similar to that in most English parish churches. (Indeed it seems to be in the 1890s that the term "English church" first began to be applied locally to St. Andrew's). One small but very significant difference was restored in 1897 when it was agreed that the old Scottish liturgy should be used on those Sundays when there was also a celebration according to the Prayer Book. Most of the prejudices against ritual and ornaments had been broken down. A Sunday school flourished. "Hymns Ancient and Modern" was the normal form of congregational praise. Services were choral, and evening services were fully accepted. After 1890 the incumbent began to be styled "rector" and the beadle was renamed "verger", though the one lacked teinds and the other a rod.

In 1893 Mr. Tuttiett retired, reluctantly, after twenty three years service. For his last two years as rector he had been assisted by a curate, Mr. P. Minos, the first of a long line of young men who gained in St. Andrews their first experience of parochial work. To his successor Mr. Tuttiett left a large, and growing congregation, and a church in good shape financially. To Christians everywhere he left his many devotional writings such as "Plain forms of household prayers" and "Services and readings in prolonged sickness", as well as many hymns of which two survive in "Hymns Ancient and Modern" – "Father let me dedicate all this year to thee" and "O quickly come dread judge of all".

His successor was the Reverend Ithel Owen, Curate of Hallow, Henwick, chosen by the vestry from some hundred and fifty applicants, a number which tells much of the standing of the charge.

CHAPTER 6

Under the leadership of Mr. Owen and his successor there began a building programme which astonishes us today. Within ten years the vision, the courage and the wealth of the congregation made possible the erection of the church–hall, of the rectory, of St. Saviour's mission church in Guardbridge and of the first iron church of All Saints.

The hall and the vestries had long been necessary. The clergy and choir lacked robing rooms, the clergy having to make do with a small area partitioned off from the north transept and the choir with the ten foot by six foot space behind the organ. The Sunday School, for a time at least, had to meet in the Town Hall. Above all the congregation lacked a place for social activities. Mr. MacGregor again proved a generous benefactor, offering to sell for £450 the ground to the west of the church over which he had earlier given the vestry a servitude, a piece of ground stretching north from Queen's Terrace for some four hundred feet. His offer was quickly accepted, the vestry seeing that the ground was sufficient not only for a hall but also for the rectory which they hoped to build once the necessary funds were available.

Approval for the building of the "church room", as the hall was originally called, and vestries was given at a congregational meeting in July 1893 and an appeal for money was launched. David Henry, the architect of the Burgh School and the Gibson Hospital, was chosen as architect. The building work was carried out with the enviable speed of most 19th century building, so that the bishop could dedicate the finished work in July 1895. The architect was sympathetic in his design and material, conforming to the style of the church building and using matching stone from Strathkinness. He was constrained by the west window in church which made it necessary to provide a flat roof to the adjoining part of the new building. The total cost was a little more than one thousand pounds, met partly by immediate fund–raising efforts and subscriptions, partly by the money which Bishop Wordsworth had dissuaded the congregation from spending on a spire.

The fund–raising efforts which brought in a not inconsiderable part of the money for all the building of the period were chiefly bazaars and sales–of–work organised and run mainly by the ladies of the congregation, many of whom enjoyed both wealth and the leisure provided by domestic servants. One of these bazaars, held in the Town Hall in 1903, may serve as an example of what was done and what was achieved. The theme of the bazaar was suggested by the Delhi Durbar, the great gathering of princely rulers of India to greet the

Prince of Wales. The Town Hall was decorated in Indian style for three days. There were stalls of all sorts including one which offered sportsmen's material – Singer's patent Golf Balls, clubs. cleeks, cartridge cases and the like. There were performances of "Cox and Box" and "Chalk and Cheese". Each day the bazaar was formally opened, on the first day by H.T. Anstruther M.P., on the second by the dowager countess of Limerick, and on the third day by Lady Ida Low. £702 was raised and at a later sale of the surplus another £102. It is impossible to give an exact equivalent of this £804 in the money of 1988, but it is interesting to note that Mr. McGregor's wages book of the time shows that skilled cabinet–makers were paid £75 a year, and that the rector might have posted 480 Christmas cards for one pound.

The next major building was the rectory. After the parsonage in Playfair Terrace was sold when the new church was built, the incumbent was left to rent a house privately, receiving from the vestry in lieu an annual payment, which rose to £60 by the end of the renting. Mr. Owen, for example, rented 4 Dempster Terrace. It was not a very satisfactory arrangement. The vestry decided to build a rectory which would be close to the church and be large enough to house a Victorian family, to accommodate the necessary domestic staff and to give the rector a study. The ground earlier bought from Mr. Mcgregor gave ample room for the house, the approach drive and a garden. The commission for the building and layout of the ground was given to Messrs. Gillespie and Scott, the architects who had been established since the early 1880s. (Happily in the person of the secretary to vestry, Mr. J.L.H. Scott the church and architects are still closely linked). Their design provided the congregation, and the town, with a building of distinction – "Late Gothic adaptation of the cottage style, severe in mood, with over–hanging eaves, prominent wooden barge–boards and steeply pitched gables". The estimated cost was £2,345.

When this new rectory was ready for occupation in 1897 the vestry had completed its building work on the Queen's Terrace site, having created a group of buildings commensurate with the size and the standing in the town of the congregation. Fortunately, they could not foresee how great a burden their works were to be to their successors.

During all this building activity the rector was not unmindful of the spiritual needs of episcopalians outwith St. Andrews. By 1896 a small congregation was forming in Guardbridge, where in February, in a bare room, a group of sixteen met for Matins and Holy Communion. By a happy chance the altar of the old North Street church was used then and later. When that church was sold the altar had been sold to a member of the vestry. Oliphant wrote indignantly: "It is startling to find that a then member of the vestry became possessed of the altar, apparently without protest from anyone, and converted it into a lobby table, having first had the legs taken out and turned to match the rest of his furniture".

St. Saviour's, Guardbridge

The worshippers came from Strathkinness as well as from Guardbridge and Leuchars. Their pious enthusiasm encouraged the vestry to build a small Mission Church which was consecrated on March 24th 1901, St. Saviour's Church. At first the mission was served from St. Andrews by the rector or the curate, on whom it imposed a considerable burden at a time when there was no means of transport to Guardbridge on Sundays, other than bicycle or horse–drawn vehicle. There were perils too, on the way. The service book in 1899 notes: "There was no service on the 23rd (of June) on account of a carriage accident which happened to the Rector on his way to Guardbridge. By the good providence of God he was not injured." Morning services were sometimes very early. On Easter Sunday in 1906 Holy Communion was celebrated at 6.20 a.m. when 22 communicants were present, including 7 from Strathkinness, nearly all of them mill–workers. Congregations in these days were never large, seldom more than 25 at Evensong which was usually better attended than Matins.

There was a real need for a resident leader in Guardbridge to take the regular services, to run a Sunday school, and to be a pastor. In 1904 Mr. A.J. Hall was licensed as lay reader, the first in a succession of stipendiary lay readers who were to serve the congregation till the 1920s. He was an energetic man of vision who tried to extend the work in Guardbridge by establishing a mission in Strathkinness. In the year of his appointment he began to hold services in the Mitchell Hall there, services attended by a few faithful worshippers.

The mission work was supplemented by a Band of Hope which attracted 18 young people. Sadly the mission was short lived. By August 1906 it ceased, for reasons which are not clear.

In 1870 there were some 800 inhabited houses in St. Andrews. By 1904 there were 1574, many of them large villas or spacious terrace houses such as those in Hope Street or Howard Place. The increase in the population which made this staggering increase necessary had serious consequences for the church: it proved to be too small to house the congregation at major festivals. Numbers were swollen too, by the arrival of girls from St. Leonards School after it opened in 1877, and by boys from St. Salvator's and Clifton Bank school By 1902 for example, girls from St. Leonards and St. Katherines occupied 153 of the sittings. In that year the congregational magazine reported. "There are over 100 resident communicants who have no sittings in the church in which nearly every seat is let and there are 80 children in our Sunday School for whom we can provide no accommodation at our Sunday morning service."

Ways of overcoming the difficulty were considered by the vestry. The first was by enlarging the church, extending it on the north side to give an additional 183 sittings. The other was by building a mission church at the east end of North Street, the fisher quarter at the Lady Head where mission work among the poor had been carried out for some time. A plebiscite of the congregation was held to decide which course to follow. The response was not very satisfactory. The voting showed:

8 in favour of extending the church
30 in favour of a stone–built mission church
40 in favour of an iron mission church
47 in favour of holding two services every Sunday
82 in favour of doing nothing.

The vestry wisely ignored the conservative majority and decided to build an iron church on part of the ground on which the present All Saints' Church now stands. In May 1903 this small church, supplied by the firm of Spiers of Glasgow, was consecrated, offering seating to 150 worshippers. In it all sittings were free and unappropriated, a church:

"Where the poor man, meanly dressed
Is as welcome as the best;
And rich and poor may gather
Kneeling to their common Father."

to quote T.T Oliphant who hated the social divisions in the congregation caused by seat rents and worked hard to have the Mission Church built. In his memory a fund was started to build a stone chancel. This was completed and dedicated in 1907.

The history of All Saints' Church and congregation, which became independent in 1920, is to be found in Judith W. George's "All Saints' Church, St. Andrews" and I need add little to what she has written.

The Sunday services were timed to fit in with those of the mother church. The eucharist in St. Andrew's at 8 a.m. followed by the eucharist in All Saints at 9.45 a.m.: Evensong in St. Andrew's at 6 p.m. was followed by Evensong in All Saints at 7 p.m. Attached to All Saints there was a flourishing Men's Institute where Temperance reigned – a virtue understandably lacking in the poor housing of the area where the public house offered warmth, light, comfort and company. A glimpse of what happened there is found in the "Citizen" of 1908 which tells how on Old Year's Night members of the Institute met for supper. After supper they enjoyed a lantern–lecture by the rector on mission work in South Africa, followed by songs and recitations till midnight, when they all adjourned to the church where twenty one members took the pledge of total abstinence in the presence of a crowded congregation.

This chapter has been much taken up with stone and mortar and money. The other and more important work of the church is best described in another brief note in the "Citizen".

"The Episcopal Church is sometimes held to be the Church of the rich and cultured, but no Christian body works more faithfully among the poor in St. Andrews than the Episcopal Church. The clergy and lay visitors will be found faithfully in the poorer quarters of the city at all times."

71

Charitable and mission work was not confined to St. Andrews. In 1899 Mr. Owen resigned his charge to become incumbent of Oldswinford. (The patron was Lord Dudley who was a regular autumn visitor to St. Andrews). The Reverend Edward Winter, Rector of King's Lynn, was Mr. Owen's successor. He saw the need for the congregation, and indeed, the Church to reach out in mission work. The Boer War had made many people at home aware of the complexities of South African social relationships. In particular the Churches had been made to realise that the large, non–white population needed all the spiritual and material help it was possible to give them. In the mission work undertaken by the Scottish Episcopal Church in South Africa Canon Winter was an enthusiastic worker. He spent months there in 1904 coming home to act as an energetic propagandist, both locally and nationally. The congregation supported him with their purses, in 1905 giving £93 to foreign missions including the mission to Africa, Kaffraria, and the Umtata Cathedral Fund, as well as £53 to such home charities as the Aberlour Orphanage,the Perth Home for Girls and the Church Penitentiary work. Inevitably the outbreak of war in 1914 restricted the missionary outreach, but did not end it. The eyes of congregations had been lifted from their narrow parochial view and were to remain lifted.

When he relinquished the charge in 1916 Canon Winter left a congregation solidly founded and solidly funded with two flourishing mission churches, though all sadly stripped of their young men, too many of whom were not to return. The

72

roots were strong in the Sunday School where Miss Houston the superintendent, had ninety children under her care. The abstract of accounts for the year ending 1915 show that there was an income of £442 from pew rents and £442 from offertories which, with interest and credit balance gave a total of £923. This sufficed to pay the curate £150, the verger £52, the rector £380, coal gas and electricity £33 and choir expenses of £145, as well as to provide for contributions to missions and charities and all the minor running expenses of the church. (There was a new and ominous payment to be made that year – fifteen guineas for "aircraft and bombardment insurance").

Treasurers' accounts can tell us nothing about the spiritual life of the congregation, but they do tell us that in 1915 there was a large group of worshippers to support those who in the grim years to come were to need all the support and solace that could be given them.

CHAPTER 7

Canon Winter was succeeded by the Reverend George Nowell Price, the headmaster of Loretto Junior School. In spite of the fact that he had spent almost all his priesthood as a schoolmaster – from 1900 to 1907 at Sandroyd School, and from 1908 to 1911 at Loretto – Mr. Price settled quickly into parochial work in the difficult conditions of wartime when he had no curate to help him in maintaining services in the three places of worship in his charge. Occasional help came from retired clergy but the burden was his. In the months between the departure of Canon Winter and November when Mr. Price was inducted Canon Parry came from the Theological College to act as priest–in–charge.

War–work of all sorts absorbed much of the energy of the congregation. The armed forces took the young men. Women undertooka vast number of onerous duties. Many left the town temporarily to do this work. By 1919 the congregation was coming together again, welcoming back the wanderers and planning how best to commemorate its dead. It was decided that the memorial should be one that all could see at every service, that the chancel should become that memorial. Dr. McGregor Chalmers prepared a design for the work which consisted of lining the chancel with dressed arcaded stone work, on the south wall of which a brass plate recording the names of the fallen was placed. On November 5th 1922 Brigadier General Grogan unveiled it, speaking with moving eloquence to a congregation which knew that two Grogan names were recorded on the memorial tablet.

By 1922 a major change had taken place in the life of the congregation. Mrs. Younger of Mount Melville, the present day Craigtoun, a devout and generous church woman, had created two trusts. By one she gave £26,000 to endow All Saints' as a separate church, where the Scottish liturgy should be used. By the other she gave £2,600 to St. Andrew's, the interest from which was to be used to help pay the stipend of the curate. The vestry agreed to accept the endowment and the conditions. In 1920 the Reverend P. A. Wilson became priest–in–charge of All Saints. In 1930 the charge became completely independent with Mr. Wilson as rector. The town was divided into two episcopal parishes, so permitting each congregation to have its own representative in diocesan matters. The division did not and does not in any way restrict the freedom of worshippers who are welcome in either church wherever they live. The parish boundary is an administrative convenience.

Until 1930s women had no role in services in church. They were the Marthas of the congregation, very industrious, very necessary.

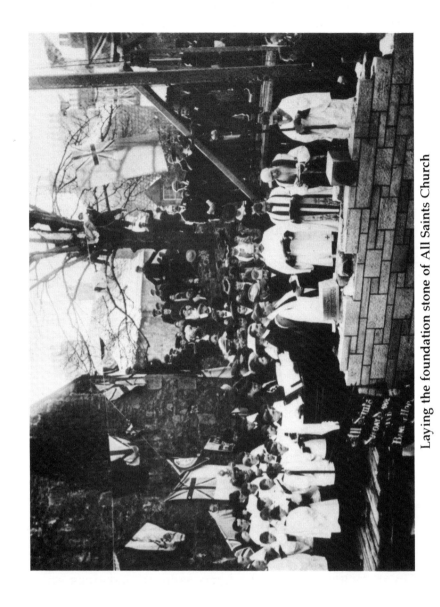

Laying the foundation stone of All Saints Church

They had raised enormous sums of money; they had been greatly involved in charitable works; they had seen to the flowers; they had done much to add to and tend vestments; and they were hostesses. All these things they still do, and more, much more.

Music first gave a few a role in public worship. In 1928 Mr. Freeman, the organist, retired after fifty year's service. His successor found the choir weak in alto voices and asked permission of the vestry to use female voices. Consent was given grudgingly. She was allowed to use female voices, provided that they did not enter nor sit with the choir but occupied a pew in the north transept behind the choir. It proved to be an unworkable arrangement and in 1922 the singers were permitted to sit in the choir, provided that they wore both black gowns and Oxford caps. It was a decision for which we have cause to be grateful. As the number of boys willing and able to submit themselves to the discipline of choristers declined the choir had to rely more and more on women. The decision was important in another way. The congregation became accustomed to women taking an active part in services.

One appointment made during Mr. Price's incumbency deserves a special note. In 1934 the vestry appointed Mr. Harry Studley as verger. For the next thirty years his dignified, begowned presence at the church door seemed an essential part of Sunday services. When ill health forced him to retire the congregation felt that an old and valued friend had left them.

Mr. Price died a few days before Christmas in 1934 after a sudden seizure while taking a service in Guardbridge, mourned by his own Church people and by a great number of others, for he had given a great deal of his free time to service in the community. He had been a Justice of the Peace, chairman of the old Parish Council, a member of the School Board, president of the Musical Association and even president of the Burns Club. His enthusiasm for games led him into the Royal and Ancient and into the Curling Club of which he served his time as president. In addition to all this voluntary work he and Mrs. Price conducted for a time a preparatory school in the rectory, a school for both boys and girls. There were two class rooms, one in the basement for beginners, on upstairs for the seniors.[12]

In all these varied ways he entered fully into the work and play of the town. All this when his rectorial duties were heavy. In the 1930s there was no layreader in Guardbridge and the pastoral care of that congregation as well as the conduct of services there had to be shared between him and the curate. On the first Sunday of each month he celebrated Holy Communion in St. Saviour's and on the other Sundays on the month he conducted Evensong with a sermon. In St. Andrews a large congregation demanded much care and tact. The High Altar is the congregation's memorial to him.

In a choice of a successor to Mr. Price the vestry was very successful. They appointed the Reverend William Shaw Andrew, Rector of Ingham and Culford Heath, whose ministry guided the congregation through the troubled years of war and through the beginning of the very difficult years that followed. For much of the time he was guide not to this congregation only, for his administrative ability and his diplomacy led to his being chosen as dean, an onerous office which he held from 1943 to 1959, giving all the diocese the benefit of his wisdom and experience. His wartime experience as Chaplain in the 1914–18 war, where he won his Military Cross, gave him an affection for Scotland and Scots people which prompted him to come here. In the minds of all who remember him he remains the much–loved model of a rector of the old school, very diligent in pastoral work and very careful to preserve the solemn dignity of the services.

He came on a building problem which threatened to be very expensive. The tower was beginning to shed plaster and develop cracks as it began to lean towards the Kinnessburn. The firm of the original architects, Rowand Anderson and Balfour Paul was consulted and the advice of the professor of geology and others was sought. Demolition was recommended, especially when it seemed that the movement of the tower threatened to crack the chancel arch. The cost of demolition, £1079, was met mainly by the response to a thousand letters of appeal and a notice in the St. Leonards School "Gazette". In 1938 the tower was reduced to the level of the chancel eaves and St. Andrews was deprived of a land mark.

The war brought other problems with buildings. In 1940 the church hall and the choir vestry were requisitioned by the army. A year later the requisitioning was extended to the rectory, to be used first by the women of the A.T.S., later by Polish officers. The substantial iron railings and gates which surrounded the church were removed for smelting. Even the trees were sacrificed to the war effort. The trees on the south side which overshadowed Queen's Terrace harboured rooks, which were accused of damaging crops. To remove their nesting sites all except the trees at the east and at the west were felled. After the war small sums were paid as compensation for the railings and for the wear and tear of the buildings, "barrack damages", but not sufficient to pay for replacing the railings or making good all dilapidation. One benefit came from the rector's temporary eviction from the rectory. He and the vestry came to realise that the rectory was vastly too big. After the war Mr. A.G. Scott prepared plans to cut off the basement and turn it into a separate flat, which which was completed by 1946. It was not a prefect solution, for the large house that remained became increasingly difficult to heat and run.

During these war years two important decisions were made, one affecting the administration, the other the finances of the church. In 1944 a special General Meeting of the congregation agreed that women might serve as members of the vestry and the constitution was amended accordingly. (One male member of the congregation was not happy, for he disapproved of women taking up the collection. Mrs. Williams, a leader of the women's petition for admission, assured him that no lady would want to do so). The decision permitted Dr. Guild to become the first woman member of the vestry, the first of many who have served since then. This was the first major step towards permitting women to share equally in the offices and duties of the church.

From the beginning the church had relied for a large part of its income on pew rents. For the treasurer it was an admirable system. The rents were easy to collect and they provided him with a substantial sum at the beginning of each year, or quarter, as well as giving him some indication of what the total income for the year would be. Socially it was now outmoded and in wartime it was ill suited to a fluctuating congregation. In 1944, on the initiative of Dr. H. Richardson, the vestry clerk, a system of covenants was introduced. Finally in 1963 the pew rents were abolished and seats became free for all. (A few traces of the old system remain in the card–holders fixed at the ends of some pews).

Dean Andrew retired at the end of September 1960 leaving a congregation which was devoted to him for all his qualities as a man and as a priest and for all his pastoral care during his long ministry. The memory of that ministry is kept alive by three windows in church. He is commemorated by the window in the north wall of the chancel, his first wife by the window of the Lady Chapel. The Chapel, which was created in 1945, is both a memorial and a thank offering, for the heart of it is the altar which was given by the Norwegian servicemen who had worshipped in church during their wartime stay with us.

In 1993 the third window, a memorial to the second Mrs. Andrew, was placed in the south wall of the nave.

The 25 years after Dean Andrew's departure was a difficult time for the church. They were the years of the rebellious young. It is still hard to understand what caused and what fed the rebellion. When it first manifested itself in pseudo–Edwardian dress and hairstyle it was assumed that this was no more than the modern version of the post–war exhibitionism of the 1920s – the shingle, the Oxford bags, the Charleston and the rest – and that the young would soon settle down. They failed to do so and went on to create a sub–culture that rejected the beliefs, the morals, the manners and the institutions of their parents and summed up its philosophy in the phrase "Do your own thing". The phrase proclaimed an unchristian attitude to life, making selfishness and disregard for one's neighbour acceptable. This is not the place for a long digression on the nature of our society in the 1960s and 1970s but two things must be stressed. The first is that to many young people then the Church as an institution and its form of worship became irrelevant. The other is that these young people of the 60s are now the middle–aged parents of the 90s who have retained the outlook of their youth.

Financially too, this was a difficult time. Steadily increasing inflation diminished the wealth of those members of the congregation who lived on fixed incomes. Professional incomes declined relatively. The cost of everything needful in church, from rectorial stipend to altar candles, increased year by year.

Yet this quarter century was also a time when profound changes began to be made in the liturgical forms of service and in the role of the laity in the whole life of the church. The Second Vatican Council began its deliberations in 1962, examining most aspects of the Roman Catholic Church and making recommendations of a revolutionary nature. The discussions of the Council and the decisions reached had a very strong influence on churches of the Anglican communion.

The rector who succeeded Dean Andrew was the Reverend John Scott (Canon Scott after 1962), coming to us from Bridge of Allan, a man well suited to lead the congregation through the troubled years ahead. He was already experienced in parish work when he came, and had learned much about human nature during his years of service as a wartime chaplain in the Royal Air Force. That wartime service helped him to keep in touch with the world of teenagers in St. Andrews where he acted as chaplain to the Air Training

Corps. His understanding of the changing modes of adolescents was further helped by his two school–girl daughters who kept him in touch with the idioms and cults of their generation. Indeed it seemed that the church had acquired with the rector a rectorial team, for Mrs. Scott became much involved in the work of the Sunday School and in innumerable other forms of church activity, while,for a time, his elder daughter Janet, led a group of under 25s. To the changes in the form of worship with which the Episcopal Church experimented he was open–minded, but conservatively prudent, careful to take the congregation with him.

During most of his ministry financial worries were never far away. Even before he came in 1958 house–to–house visiting by a team from the congregation asking for increased giving had been found necessary. The abolition of pew rents in 1963 made another money–raising campaign necessary and by 1970 it was clear that expenditure had to be reduced. Various proposals were made – that St. Saviour's Church in Guardbridge should be closed; that we should unite with All Saints' Church; that the Chaplaincy to Anglican students should not be a charge on the congregation. In 1971 a firm decision to close and sell St. Saviour's was taken. It was finally sold for some £1750 and converted into a private house. Even with this supplement the vestry found it necessary to arrange another house–to–house appeal in 1972. Economy, good management and increased giving enabled the treasurer to show a small surplus in 1974 but the battle against rising costs continued throughout the early 70s. Some cash was raised by the sale of surplus church ornaments – the antique chalice and an alabaster panel from St. Saviour's, and furnishings – a grandfather clock, a corner cupboard and a painting of the "Deposition from the Cross" – from St. Andrew's.

Despite the shortage of money much was done to make the church buildings better for worship and for social life. In 1962 the vestry decided to create a new choir vestry by making a new room over the northern third of the hall. This made it possible to turn the old vestry into the present kitchen, to the very great benefit of the social life of the congregation – the source of after–service coffee, Harvest Festival lunches, of Garden Fete tea, of refreshments generally. In the same year the rectory flat which had been let, became vacant. Instead of reletting it the vestry decided to use it for church purposes, making it available for meetings of the newly formed "Under 25" group and for one of the five classes in the Sunday School (Young Church after 1963). By 1967 the organ needed overhauling and rebuilding, at great cost, some £9000, almost half of which was given by one member of the congregation. The work was carried out under the expert guidance, freely given, of Mr. Tom Duncan, the organist of Holy Trinity Church. The re–modelling made it possible to create the present sacristy.

It may seem that too much attention has been paid in this short history to buildings and furnishings.

Such things are important, more important than is generally thought. Men and women may meet to worship God in the bare simplicity of a Free Presbyterian church, or a Cistercian cloister, finding no need of external aids to devotion, but our human frailty too often requires such aids to devotion. Architecture, music, colour, ritual, physical comfort can all provide this, and in social gatherings people learn to know and love their neighbour.

During Canon Scott's ministry the changes in forms and patterns of worship led both to greater involvement of the laity, women as well as men, and the restoration òf the eucharist to its central place. In the Church of England at this time much thought was being given to modernising the form of service, a labour from which the Alternative Service Book eventually emerged. In Scotland change came at first more conservatively and more slowly. The first of the new Scottish liturgies, the Grey Book, appeared in 1970. It was acceptable to many because it kept the language of the 1929 Prayer Book, but not to all, for some saw no need for innovation and others found it too "High". At St. Andrew's a development at this time was the start of the Family Eucharist or Parish Communion. This was a service held before the regular 11 o'clock service, at ten o'clock or earlier, inspired by the wish of some parents to have a service which would supplement the teaching in the Children's Church, by allowing children to participate in a form of the eucharist, where they could share in the celebration with their parents.

The bishop viewed the new service favourably and authorised lay members to administer the cup at it. The experiment was not without risk. If it had continued too long the congregation might have split into traditionalists at 11 a.m. and the modernisers at 9.30 a.m. But the gains were big. The laity was more involved in the service than ever before, and traditionalists came to realise that modern English and children's voices need not in any way lessen the dignity of the eucharist. The way was being prepared for to–day's unified service.

Ill health compelled Canon Scott to retire in 1978. For a time he remained in St. Andrews where, in retirement, he could see that his courage and patient leadership had brought the congregation through the worst of the 60s and 70s.

CHAPTER 8

Arguments about when "history" ends and "current affairs" begin are unavoidable. The threshold is a wide one. By 1978 it has been certainly crossed, for so much of what has happened since then is known at first hand to many of the congregation, some of whom have played important parts in the events. Increasingly the writer has to rely on memories, his own and others', and to be discreet and very brief.

Canon Scott was succeeded by the Reverend Hugh Magee, a Yale graduate, whose previous experience of ministry in Scotland had been in Dundee where he served as a member of a team of clergy based on the Cathedral. There his understanding of the problems and difficulties of adolescents, and his warm sympathy in personal relationships made him highly regarded. Yet his period in St. Andrews was not altogether a successful time. Much was asked of him. Lacking experience of parish work he had to acquire at once the diplomatic skills needed to hold together and lead a congregation containing members of varying opinions and strong minds. His difficulties were increased by the bishop's decision to link together in a loose union the congregations of St. Andrews, Elie and Pittenweem over which he had a general oversight. (The three fishes on the Church's magazine, "The Net", remind us of the union). It was a task that would have taxed an experienced priest, and one which, while it lasted, distracted some of his attention from St. Andrew's. Money problems remained and differences with the vestry over a range of subjects became increasingly sharp as the years passed. In 1983 he was happy to leave St. Andrews to become rector of Forfar.

Of his time in St. Andrews a lasting memorial remains – St. Saviour's Chapel. The altar from the North St. Church had been restored in St. Saviour's in Guardbridge. It was re–erected at the east end of the south aisle and rededicated, to become the focus of the new chapel. (The rededication caused controversy. Some of the congregation objected to the censing of the altar).

With the appointment as rector of the Reverend Robert Halliday, rector of Holy Cross Church in Edinburgh a renewal of the congregation began. He was not a stranger to St. Andrews where he served his curacy under Dean Andrew and where he was ordained priest in 1957. He was welcomed back by all who knew him as a curate. He came well experienced in parish work, familiar with the activities of church councils, radiating cheerfulness, an administrator of vision, utterly serious in all that affected the Church but never solemn, the first Scottish ordained priest since 1832 or earlier to serve St. Andrew's Church.

His ministry began with blunt words, telling the congregation that if it was to survive and flourish every member had to work, that passive goodwill was not enough. The words were followed by action. Volunteers were found for every task or service, regardless of age or sex – readers of scripture, cleaners, coffee–makers and servers, groundsmen and grounds women, welcomers at the door, book distributors and many others. In the service he involved lay men and women, establishing a "team" to act as "deacons" and "sub–deacons". Under his guidance some laymen were encouraged to seek ordination as non–stipendiary priests, to serve both this and other congregations, and women to be ordained as deacons.

To the main Sunday services he brought unity, bringing together the 11 o'clock and the Family Eucharist Services at 10 o'clock. In this joint service the 1970 liturgy and the modern language Blue Book, which was published in 1982 were used alternately, as were the high altar and a nave altar previously in the private chapel of Bishop Carey of Edinburgh. [This altar is now at the mission church of St. Mary–in–the–Fields, Culloden]. Matins remained on one Sunday in the month, but the pre–eminence of eucharistic worship was firmly established.

Practical improvements were made to the buildings. An amplifying system was installed to overcome the acoustic problems of the church. A ramp was made to allow wheelchair access to service. The rectory was divided into two flats to give future rectors a more manageable home in the lower flat, and the vestry some money from the sale of the upper.

All these changes had one end in view – to quicken the spiritual lives of the congregation, to make growth in faith and devotion more vigorous. To this end the question, "What is the purpose of this church" was discussed prayerfully in house groups, in team meetings, in vestry meetings, in a long mission. The definition of the purposes of this church – worship, binding people together in God's family, outreach in witness and in caring – led to much thinking and discussion about how the congregation could work to achieve these purposes. There could be no final answer. Thinking continues and action follows. There is no way of telling how each member of the congregation has been enriched spiritually by involvement in this searching. We can judge by externals only, and the judgement is subjective. We can, however, say that when Mr. Halliday left in 1990 to become Bishop of Brechin he left a congregation where the number of communicants and the frequency of communions were yearly increasing; where there was new warmth of fellowship among the members; where there was increasing involvement in work to help the disadvantaged.

Bishop Halliday was succeeded by Dr. R.A. Gillies, the chaplain to the University of Dundee. Here this brief narrative must end for it would be an impertinence to write about a priest to whom the author owes so much and about a congregation of his friends.

NOTES

1   For a fuller background:
"An ecclesiastical history of Scotland." George Grub
"A short history of the Scottish Episcopal Church" Frederick Goldie
"Religious life in Scotland in the Seventeenth Century" G.D. Henderson
"Scottish Church History" G. Donaldson

2   MS in university library.

3   The so-called "Laud's Liturgy", which occasioned a riot when it was first used in St. Giles' Cathedral.

4   MS in university library.

5   W.Croft Dickinson in "Two Students in St. Andrews 1711–1716." Edited Morice's letters to the Mackenzie boys' parents. From them he appears as a very conscientious, rather fussy tutor.

6   "Diary of a tour in 1732"

7   "The transcript of the register of baptisms, Muthill from 1697–1847"

8   "Poems with a preface by the editor" – Mrs. Elizabeth Berkeley. In her long preface to her son's

93

poems Mrs. Berkeley gives a fair amount of information about St. Andrews.

9 James Boswell – "The Journal of the Tour of the Hebrides".

10 William Robb – "Poems illustrative of the genius and influence of Christianity".

11 The old church was sold to the congregation of the Free Church in Buckhaven. It was demolished stone by stone, shipped to Buckhaven and re-erected there. The building, with some alterations, is now used as a theatre.

12 An article by Miss Elizabeth Bushnell in the "Net" of September 1991 gives a pupil's memories of this school.

POSTSCRIPT

On Thursday 18th November 1993 Dr. John Thompson delivered the completed manuscript of his history of Saint Andrew's Church to Mrs. Sybil Davis. It was her task to commit it to type. The next evening Dr. Thompson collapsed and died at his home, Blackfriars.

Such was his sense of completeness that he had returned all the material upon which he had been working to the Church that same week.

An unposted letter to one of his daughters was found at Blackfriars. It contained the following: "The pocket history of St. Andrew's Episcopal Church is off for its final word processing. It is (and I speak with no false modesty) so bad that I'll see if I can alter the title page from 'by J. Thompson' to 'by a member of the congregation.'"

In the <u>Net</u> for October 1993 and in my Rector's Annual Report for 1993, I had signalled the near completion of Dr. Thompson's text. It was very widely known he was writing the volume. Equally, he knew I would not have allowed him to write anonymously. His family concur with me and therefore his name remains where it should proudly be.

In addition Dr. Thompson and I had discussed publication details. I would seek a publisher for only a very limited print run, some four hundred copies. Three hundred paperback for the congregation, a few hardback for the family, University Library, Town Library, and the church. The remainder to be sold as quickly as possible.

The text within these covers is, with only minor typographical corrections, Dr. Thompson's. Two further acknowledgements should be made; to Mrs. Sybil Davis for typing the finished book to camera–ready standard and to Miss Aylwin Clark for proof–reading the final script.

R.A. Gillies
St. Andrews
January 1994